The Path to Green Investing

A Buddha-Inspired Guide

Table of Contents

Chapter 1. Introduction

Welcome to a transformative journey that beautifully marries ancient wisdom and modern economy! Our special report, "The Path to Green Investing: A Buddha-Inspired Guide" is a unique perspective on conscientious wealth creation. Venture down a path less trodden, where sustainable investments and mindfulness intersect. Through this special report, you'll delve into the compelling world of green investing with the serene touch of Buddhist principles. Guided by wellness for both our world and wallets, our meticulously researched guide enlightens you on how to shape an investment portfolio that's not just profitable, but compassionate and sustainable. With each page turned, you will discover how to interweave the tranquility of Buddha's teachings into the dynamic sphere of green investing. This is the reading experience you weren't expecting, but certainly the one you need. Get ready to illuminate your investment journey with wisdom from time immemorial, tailored for the challenges of today. Whether you're a seasoned investor or a newfound enthusiast, this absorbing narrative is sure to inspire. Let's together traverse this Path to Green Investing!

Chapter 2. Introducing Green Investing: A New Generation Of Wealth

The sun casts a golden hue over the landscape, teasing the leaves of a rich, verdant forest. They sway in the caress of the wind, harmoniously coexisting with the earth. This is the beauty of nature, untouched, thriving in its raw element — the emblem of sustainable living. Just as the sun nurtures the forest, so can our investments. The two can lead to remarkable growth; the only difference is that the latter requires human intervention. Just as we sow and reap fruits from trees, the seeds of investments, when sown wisely, yield rich returns. From this organic metaphor emerges a new, conscientious perspective on investing—Green Investing.

2.1. The Concept of Green Investing

Before we delve into the depths of Green Investing, let's start at the roots. At its core, Green Investing, also known as sustainable or ethical investing, forms a part of Socially Responsible Investing (SRI). SRI encapsulates any investment strategy seeking both financial returns and positive societal impact. It is a broad umbrella under which Green Investing finds its home.

Drilling it down, Green Investing is the practice of investing in companies and technologies committed to the well-being of the environment. The goal is twofold—seeking profit-making opportunities and encouraging a healthier planet. It analyses the environmental footprint of potential investments to ascertain their green status. Hence, it places a hefty emphasis on environmental due diligence.

2.2. Shift from Traditional to Green Investing

In the traditional sense, investing focused primarily on financial returns. Its primary currency was the prospect of growing wealth. However, as societal consciousness has evolved, an increasing number of investors are seeking out investments that also yield social and environmental benefits. 'Profit at any cost' is transitioning to 'profit with purpose'. This is where Green Investing comes into play.

Green Investing isn't just an economic shift; it represents a social and cultural transformation that redefines the value of wealth. Our money can now act as agents of change, creating a positive environmental impact. Investments reflect the values of the investor, and this shift is a testament that more people value maintaining the Earth's health.

2.3. The Green Economy

The Green Economy is steadily gaining prominence, driven by recognition of the imminent climate crisis. Companies worldwide are shifting towards sustainable operations platforms to reduce carbon footprints. Governments are implementing green initiatives and formulating regulations, thus encouraging this transition. It's contributing to the creation of a new paradigm for economic growth, employment, and wealth creation—all within environmental limits.

On the corporate front, adhering to green principles increases reputation and customer desirability while reducing the risks from stricter regulations. On a consumer level, people increasingly prefer green products and are more likely to support businesses that respect the environment. This amalgamation of positive factors is fueling the expansion of the Green Economy, creating an ideal playground for

Green Investing.

2.4. Exploring Green Assets

The realm of possible green investments is broad and varied. It ranges across industries, from renewable energy to sustainable agriculture and beyond. Companies engaged in generating power from renewable sources such as solar, wind, and hydroelectric power offer green opportunities. So do companies committed to energy efficiency, waste management, water technology, conservation, and sustainable agriculture.

Public equities (stocks in companies with green initiatives), private equities (young green ventures needing capital), and green bonds (raised to fund projects with environmental benefits) are some examples of green assets. Green Exchange Traded Funds (ETFs) and green mutual funds are excellent opportunities to diversify holdings across several green companies.

2.5. Measuring the 'Green' in Green Investing

Green Investing isn't as straightforward as it may seem. The term 'Green' can often be misleading or misused in the realm of investing. Some companies project eco-friendly images or use environmental marketing schemes while continuing environmentally-harmful practices, a practice known as 'Greenwashing'.

To navigate this, investors need rigorous environmental due diligence. They need access to precise, standardized metrics to evaluate the environmental impact alongside the financial potential of investments. Several reporting frameworks such as Global Reporting Initiative (GRI), Sustainability Accounting Standards Board (SASB), and Task Force on Climate-related Financial Disclosures

(TCFD) provide guidance on sustainability reporting, making it easier for investors to make informed decisions.

2.6. The Changing Market Dynamics

In an era where the global economy and environment are intertwined, Green Investing comes as a breath of fresh air. Adopting sustainable measures isn't just about 'doing good'; it also aligns with 'doing well.'

Research has shown that companies committed to sustainable practices tend to have better operational performance and are less risky. Environmental, Social, and Governance (ESG) portfolios have demonstrated their ability to match or even outperform traditional portfolios.

Investors, now more than ever, are expressing appetite for investments reflecting their values without compromising on returns. They're supportive of companies that put sustainability at the heart of their business models. This alignment of investing and societal values give us the hope of a thriving future.

In conclusion, green investing is a prosperous and responsible avenue to build wealth for ourselves and our world. It's a tool of financial empowerment that extends beyond the individual to the collective community. It brings investing in line with the changing landscape of the economy and evolving social consciousness. After all, wealth isn't only about creating financial assets—it's also about enriching the world we inhabit. As we journey deeper into green investing, remember that the goal isn't to extract maximum value but to exchange value respectfully and sustainably. This is the true essence of the wealth for the new generation.

From this point on, the path ahead diverges from tradition. The road now leads us towards a unique destination, one where the landscape is green in every sense—prosperity interlaced with sustainability.

Chapter 3. Buddhist Philosophy: Timeless Wisdom For Investors

The essence of Buddhism is the understanding of the interconnectedness of all things and the incessant change they undergo. This knowledge gives rise to wisdom: the capacity to perceive reality and act accordingly. Such a perspective can be incredibly fruitful in the realm of investing, particularly green investing, which interplays economic development and environmental sustainability.

3.1. The Four Noble Truths and Investing

The fundamental teachings of the Buddha begin with the Four Noble Truths: the truth of suffering, its cause, its end, and the path leading to its end. While these tenets were aimed at the spiritual liberation of individuals, they can be extrapolated to provide guidance in the world of investing.

The first truth, Dukkha (suffering), can be equated with the environmental, social, and economic problems challenging our planet. As green investors, recognizing this suffering is the first step towards meaningful change.

The second truth, Samudaya (the cause of suffering), links suffering with attachment. In investing terms, it means that our unsustainable behaviors, driven by unchecked desire for maximum profits, are the cause of environmental and social suffering.

Nirodha, the third truth, is the cessation of suffering. This suggests that there is a way to end these issues, and with mindful, sustainable investing, we can contribute to this end.

Lastly, the fourth Noble Truth is Magga, the path leading to the cessation of suffering. This points us towards ethical and sustainable investing as the path to creating a more balanced and harmonious world.

3.2. Karma and Responsible Investing

The doctrine of Karma states that for every action, there is a reaction. This idea of consequences strongly correlates with the concept of responsible investing. When we invest in non-sustainable ventures, we contribute to the environmental and social dilemmas plaguing our world. However, when we turn towards green investing, we contribute to a sustainable future and potentially receive financial gains as an added bonus. Remember, Karma in the context of investing isn't punitive, but instructive, leading us towards wise decision making.

3.3. The Middle Way and Balanced Portfolio

The Middle Way, known as Madhyamāpratipad in Buddhism, teaches us to avoid both the extreme of indulgence in sensual pleasure and the extreme of self-mortification. In an investment portfolio, this may translate into a balance between high-risk, high-return assets and safe, low-return assets, ultimately leading to a steady, long-term growth.

3.4. Interconnectedness: Understanding System Risk

In Buddhism, the concept of 'Dependent Origination' relates to the interconnectedness and interdependency of all things. This principle applies aptly to green investing where a systemic view of risk is needed. By understanding the interconnected nature of companies, markets, societies, and the environment, investors can better anticipate and manage systemic risks — from economic downturns to climate change impacts.

3.5. Impermanence: Embracing Market Volatility

The understanding of Anicca, or Impermanence, is essential in Buddhism and perhaps even more so in the world of investing. It encourages us to embrace change, rather than resist it, and use it as an opportunity rather than a threat. This wisdom can help investors remain calm during market turbulence and make proactive adjustments, capturing new opportunities that arise from the changing market conditions.

3.6. Mindfulness and Investing

Cultivating mindfulness allows us to be more aware, enabling us to make more informed and less reactive decisions. And nowhere is this more important than in our financial choices. Through being mindful, investors can navigate the market with clarity, patience, and discernment, aligning their investments not just with financial goals, but also with their values and the broader goal of social and environmental sustainability.

By marrying Buddhist wisdom with modern investing principles, we are presented with a compassionate and wise path to wealth creation. This approach disrupts the status quo and fosters a new narrative for investing, one that places equal emphasis on societal gain and individual wealth accumulation. Remember, in the words of the Buddha, "Just as a candle cannot burn without fire, men cannot live without a spiritual life." May we all strive to intertwine our spiritual life with our worldly endeavors, illuminating the path to a sustainable and compassionate world.

Chapter 4. Awakening to Sustainable Finance: Balancing Profit and Planet

As we delve into this voyage of awakening, it is crucial to acknowledge our interconnectedness with the environment. Our every action ripples across the ecosystem, echoing beyond the confines of our immediate realities. This interconnectedness extends to the sphere of finance, where our choices significantly shape the ecological landscape.

4.1. Non-Separation: Business and Nature

All businesses ultimately rely upon natural resources. The materials meant for manufacturing come from our earth; energy to drive these processes is derived from the sun, wind, or water. Therefore, nature is not separate from business; they exist in reciprocity. As we proceed through our financial journey, it is pivotal to understand this deep connection and strive for an equilibrium that honours ecology and economy in tandem.

In his teachings, the Buddha spoke of the 'Dependent Origination' principle, which emphasizes the interdependence of all things in life. Similarly, sustainable finance recognizes that our economic activities and environmental health are intrinsically linked, obliging us to maintain this delicate balance.

4.2. Understanding Sustainable Finance

Sustainable finance, at its core, is an approach towards economic growth that takes into account ESG (Environmental, Social, and Governance) factors while ensuring adequate returns on investments. The model aims not just at minimizing negative impacts but fostering positive change through mindful decision-making. This innovative financial sector interaction model aligns closely with Buddhist principles, emphasizing compassion, mindfulness, and balanced growth.

In simpler terms, sustainable finance encourages investors and corporations to make decisions based not only on financial returns but also on how these decisions impact our society and the environment.

4.3. The Trance: Short-term Profits vs. Long-term Sustainability

Today's conventional financial metrics guide decisions based predominantly on short-term profitability. Unconsciously, we fall into the trance where immediate returns divert our attention from accounting for long-term sustainability. This selective vision can lead to the exploitation of natural resources and social inequalities.

Buddha taught the concept of mindfulness, encouraging people to be aware of their surroundings, their actions, and the consequences of their actions, breaking free from the trance. By leveraging this wisdom, we can realign our investment practices to account for long-term ecological and social implications, thus securing enduring prosperity for all.

4.4. ESG: Empathy in Numbers

ESG investing is the most common form of sustainable finance. This model encourages the evaluation of companies based on their environmental, social, and governance behaviors, alongside conventional financial analysis.

1. **Environmental Factors** assess how a company's activities affect the natural world. This could include policies related to waste management, energy use, pollution, conservation, and climate change.

2. **Social Factors** focus on the company's business relationships including those with employees, suppliers, customers, and communities where it operates. This compass points towards company values like human rights, consumer protection, employee relations and diversity, and corporate philanthropy.

3. **Governance Factors** catalogue how a corporation is managed. It includes matters like corporate risk management, corporate board diversity and structure, executive compensation, and more.

4.5. Mindful Investing: A Practitioner's Helmsmanship

As investors embark on the path of sustainable finance, they take on the role of practitioners, embracing mindfulness while navigating through investment decisions. This refined attitude involves:

1. **Empathy**: Valuing human rights and fostering equality.

2. **Compassion**: Promoting positive societal impacts.

3. **Patience**: Accepting that a sustainable approach may not offer immediate financial gratification.

4. **Resilience**: Willingness to endure potential short-term losses for long-term sustainable growth.

5. **Awareness**: Mindfully evaluating investment opportunities considering the ESG factors.

4.6. Measuring Success: The Middle Way

Buddha taught the Middle Way, a path of moderation away from the extremes of self-indulgence and self-mortification. To apply this in sustainable finance, we must shift our economic growth narrative from "growth at all costs" to one of "balanced growth."

In this paradigm, the measure of success is not merely material prosperity but our ability to foster social equality, conserve our environment, and achieve a harmonious co-existence. There will be a symbiosis between profit and planet: a lasting prosperity that leaves no one, and no thing, behind.

Our shared path towards sustainable finance serves as a testament of our capacity to imbibe timeless wisdom in addressing modern challenges. As we tread this path, let the principles and teachings of Buddha illuminate our journey, inspiring us to partake in mindful wealth creation that is in harmony with the planet we inhabit. The quest has begun: for a way of finance that nourishes the blue of the sky, the waters of the ocean, the green of the trees, and indeed, the society we dwell within.

Chapter 5. Key Concepts in Green Investing: A Primer

The path to wealth creation often leads us across myriad landscapes of investment opportunities. One such burgeoning vista of prosperity, green investing, offers a harmonious synthesis of economic progression and environmental sustenance. In the sphere of green investing, the notion of financial success beyond the quantifiable returns it yields invites us to delve deeper into the principles of sustainable, responsible, and impact investing. Our primer on this topic will serve as a wellspring of wisdom, inundating you with insights on this enlightened path to wealth generation while embodying the compassion and mindfulness integral to Buddhist teachings.

5.1. Understanding Green Investing

Green investing is a subsect of a broader, multifaceted investment approach known as sustainable, responsible, and impact investing (SRI). It focuses on investing in companies and technologies that support or provide environmentally friendly products and practices. Fundamentally, it's the application of ethical and sustainability considerations when selecting profitable investments.

This strategy champions the belief that investing should serve not only economic imperatives but also the well-being of the planet and its inhabitants. The green investing idea is influenced by a myriad of environmental, social, and governance (ESG) factors that shape the calibre and potential of an investment opportunity.

5.2. The Environmental, Social, and Governance (ESG) Framework

The ESG framework plays a quintessential role in the mechanics of green investing. These metrics evaluate a company's operational practices and influences, ensuring that investment decisions do not detrimentally impact sustainability.

1. Environmental Factors: These aspects reflect a company's stewardship of the environment and include practices concerning resource usage, pollution levels, waste management, and climate change strategies.

2. Social Factors: These criteria evaluate how a firm manages relationships with its employees, suppliers, customers, and the communities in which it operates. Critical social factors include human rights, labour standards, and community development.

3. Governance Factors: These parameters assess a company's leadership, executive pay, audits, internal controls, and shareholder rights. Governance determines a company's integrity and can significantly influence its long-term prospects.

5.3. Role of Buddhist Principles in Green Investing

The tranquil teachings of Buddhism hold immense potential when seamlessly woven into the green investing tapestry. Three cardinal tenets of Buddhism- Right Action(Avoid harm to others), Right Livelihood(Earn responsively), and Right Mindfulness(Be fully aware)- serve as the guiding beacons in the tumultuous terrains of green investing.

Green investing, at its heart, is about conscious wealth creation-making investment choices that foster a sustainable economy and environment. This alignment with Right Livelihood and Right Action ensures that financial prosperity does not come at the cost of our planet or societal harmony. Furthermore, applying Right Mindfulness encourages investors to diligently oversee their investment portfolios, ensuring their commitment remains unwavering in the face of market fluctuations.

5.4. Digging Deeper into Green Investment Types

There are several ways to engage in green investing:

1. Green Stocks: Publicly traded shares in companies engaged in environmental sectors and industries. This includes renewable energy companies, waste management firms, and eco-conscious retailers.

2. Green Bonds: These are fixed-income securities that raise capital for projects with environmental or climate benefits.

3. Green Funds: These mutual funds or ETFs invest in a portfolio of green stocks and/or bonds.

4. Impact Investing: Direct investments into companies, organizations, and funds with the intention of generating measurable environmental benefits alongside a financial return.

5.5. Assessing the Risks in Green Investing

Just as every rose has its thorns, green investing is not without risks. These investments hinge on complex and volatile areas such as alternative energy, environmental policy, and developing technology. Frequent legislative changes, technological disruptions, market adoption pace, and indirect impacts on the environment are potential sources of risk that investors should consider carefully.

However, green investing still signifies a momentous prospect to construct an investment portfolio that aligns with Buddhist principles and contributes to the global effort against climate change. Its promise of both a green planet and healthy returns makes the risks worth considering.

As you venture down this enlightening path, remember, enlightened investing is not merely about accumulating wealth but conscious wealth creation that resonates with the values inherent in you. Keep your mind open, stay aware, and make choices that contribute not only to your financial prosperity but also to the wellbeing of our world.

Chapter 6. Meditations On Risk and Reward: A Buddha-Inspired Approach

Before we embark on our journey through the prism of Buddha-inspired green investing, it is imperative to reflect on our perceptions of risk and reward. Our understanding of these concepts can affect not only our financial outcomes, but also our overall well-being and relationship with wealth creation.

6.1. Mindful Perception of Risk

Mindfulness teaches us to ground ourselves, living in the present moment rather than fretting about future uncertainties. In the realm of investing, where uncertainty often equates to risk, this perspective resonates in a profound manner.

Risk, by its financial definition, involves the probability of an investment's actual returns deviating from its anticipated returns. It evokes a sense of losing something valuable, nurturing an innate fear. Yet, borrowing from the foundational Buddhist teachings, we must understand that life is a constant flux, an interplay of ever-changing conditions. As investors, acknowledging this reality helps us accept risk as an integral part of the investment journey, rather than a terrifying specter to avoid at all costs.

The Buddha illustrated the principle of impermanence, or "anicca," reminding us of the constant change inherent in life. The market isn't a static entity; it fluctuates, it breathes and evolves. Embracing "anicca" allows us to approach investment risks with a composed mind, recognizing that fluctuations don't inherently spell disaster, but instead represent the dynamic nature of life and the economy.

Conscious mind shifts such as these transform our perspective toward risk—it becomes a fundamental truth to be acknowledged, understood, and incorporated into our investment strategy rather than an ominous shadow causing us stress and fear.

6.2. Understanding Reward Beyond Numbers

"If you propose to speak, always ask yourself, is it true, is it necessary, is it kind?" posed Buddha, emphasizing the significance of understanding and compassion over mere gain. As ethical, green investors, let's weave these words into the fabric of our investment strategy, extending the definition of 'reward' beyond mere financial return.

While it's undeniable that the core aim of investing is financial gain, a Buddha-inspired approach encourages the appreciation of broader investment outcomes. In the context of green investing, rewards manifest not only in the form of monetary returns on investments, but also through the tangible positive impact on the environment and society. The successful fruition of a social enterprise, the proliferation of clean energy, or the survival of endangered species can all form part of our reward narrative.

Mindful investing, therefore, calls on us to celebrate gains beyond the conventional sense, inspiring us toward social, moral, and environmental victories. Our portfolios, in turn, reflect not just our fiscal health, but also our contribution to a better, more sustainable world.

6.3. The Middle Way: Balancing Risk and Reward

Another core philosophy of Buddhism applicable to our investment journey is the Middle Way or "Majjhima Patipada." This concept revolves around avoiding extremes and finding a balance—an approach notably beneficial when contemplating the dichotomy of risk and reward in investing.

Green investing can represent a spectrum, with 'high risk, high reward' offerings at one end and 'low risk, low reward' vehicles at the other. The instinct might be to surrender to one extreme based on individual risk tolerance. However, a mindful approach, inspired by the Middle Way, encourages a balance.

The interplay of different investment assets, based on their risk and potential reward, leads to the constitution of a balanced portfolio. This could mean blending investment in a promising but risky start-up with a stake in a stable government green bond. This embraces both the growth prospects and the inherent instability that can accompany the green economy, forming a holistic strategy.

6.4. Cultivating Equanimity towards Risk and Reward

Buddhist teachings stress the importance of maintaining a sense of equanimity or even-mindedness, even in challenging circumstances. This idea has significant relevance to our analysis of risk and reward.

In a volatile market landscape, it's easy to surrender to the highs and lows—to celebrate exorbitantly during profitable periods and despair in times of losses. Yet, a reasoned perspective is to maintain a balanced emotional response, no matter the prevailing market conditions.

Buddha's message to us would be to learn to embrace both windfalls and downturns, understanding that each moment offers a learning experience. Whether we are reaping rewards or facing unexpected risks, our equanimity will prove a vital sanity anchor, reminding us to react with wisdom and thoughtfulness, rather than impulse.

As we progress on this conscientious journey towards green investing, employing a Buddha-inspired approach aids us in evaluating and managing risk and reward with enlightened discipline. Our decisions, aligned consciously with ancient wisdom, can lead us towards achieving sustainable and respectable returns, whilst committing to an environmentally-conscious cause. There lies the true beauty of marrying ancient principles and modern economics. Through this mindful investment approach, we grasp that besides the generation of wealth, lies the invaluable reward of purpose, satisfaction and peace amidst the financial flux.

Chapter 7. TheoZenomics: Integrating Compassion in Business Strategy

In the pantheon of concepts that bepaint the artful canvas of corporate strategy, seldom does one encounter an idea that blends spiritual wisdom with business acumen. This is the essence of TheoZenomics - an innovative integration of compassion into the lifeblood of business strategy. Rooted in the serene teachings of Buddhism, this unique approach proposes an enlightened path to long-term sustainable success.

7.1. Assimilation of Compassion

Sustainability has emerged as a key strategic pillar that many businesses achieve through environmental and social initiatives. However, going beyond compliance and philanthropy, compassion, in the Buddhist context, is a profound empathy towards the suffering of others and a genuine wish to alleviate it. This essence should fuse into the company's strategy, reframing its very purpose, governance, and processes.

Businesses are social entities that influence and are influenced by a myriad of stakeholders. A compassionate business model calls for understanding these stakeholders' plights genuinely and developing strategies catering to their wellbeing. It means considering not just stockholders, but all actors in the business ecosystem - employees, customers, suppliers, society, and even the environment.

For instance, designing products to be more accessible, affordable, and beneficial to underprivileged customers or sourcing from suppliers who respect their laborers' rights may not yield immediate financial returns. However, such steps foster goodwill, trust, and loyalty yielding long-term sustainability and responsible profitability.

7.2. Risking Compassion: The Paradox Resolved

A compelling query that arises is, 'In an inherently competitive market, how feasible is it to integrate compassion into business strategy?' This concern deserves thoughtful attention.

TheoZenomics, inspired by Buddhism, suggests a middle path - creating shared value. Shared value is a management strategy where companies not only generate economic value but concurrently advance social conditions in the communities they operate. A compassion-infused strategy is not about eradicating business competitiveness; rather, it's for seeking comprehensive stakeholder value.

Addressing this in practice can involve the reconfiguration of value chains to be more inclusive and fair, investing in the wellbeing of employees for enhanced productivity, innovating products benefiting underserved sections, or developing green technologies safeguarding the environment. These strategies pay off in improved brand reputation, customer loyalty, operational efficiencies, risk management, and innovation capacities - all augmenting the firm's market standing and long-term profitability.

7.3. The Enlightenment Perspective: Lessons from Buddhist Teachings

Buddhism offers enlightening perspectives that can be woven into business strategy, germane to fostering compassion.

1. The principle of Pratityasamutpada or Interconnectedness: This principle underscores the interconnected nature of all

phenomena. Applied to business, it prompts the understanding that businesses and stakeholders share a symbiotic relationship. Ignoring stakeholder wellbeing can eventually hinder business performance.

2. The concept of Anicca or Impermanence: This concept refers to the perpetually changing nature of life. In business terms, it counsels that clinging onto short-term profit-driven goals to the exclusion of stakeholder welfare is lacking in foresight. Businesses must be mindful of societal and environmental implications for long-term survivability.

3. The path of Samyak or Right Livelihood: This path advises that one should earn their living in a righteous, non-harming manner. Businesses should ideally operate in ways that do not exploit or harm any stakeholders.

Translating these teachings into empathetic, conscientious strategies allows businesses to build stronger, deeper connections with their stakeholders, providing a competitive edge in today's value-conscious market.

7.4. Charting a Compassionate Business Course

Becoming a compassionate business is not an overnight transformation; it is a journey requiring honest commitment and systemic change. The first step on this road is redefining business purpose to include shared value creation.

In governance, integrating compassion means setting ethical codes of conduct, aligning performance metrics and incentives with the intention to foster wellbeing, and promoting transparency. In operations, businesses can redesign value chains to become more socially and environmentally inclusive and conscious.

Moreover, compassion should imbue corporate decision-making. This involves valuing empathy and ethical accountability while brainstorming strategies and assessing performance. Annual reports can depict not just financial numbers but empathetic touchpoints reflecting a company's compassion quotient.

The path to a TheoZenomic strategy may seem challenging. However, businesses adopting this course will manifest as entities revered not merely for their profitability, but for their compassionate contribution to the world.

7.5. The Future Path

TheoZenomics is a pioneering venture, decoding a modern business strategy with wisdom from time immemorial. As we step into an era where customers, employees, and investors increasingly value ethical mindfulness, introducing compassion into strategic planning can fast-track sustainable success. It is high time businesses realized that real capital is not only what's stocked in the vault but also what's harvested in the hearts of their stakeholders.

In the profound words of Buddha, "Just as a flower does not pick and choose the bees that come to it, a compassionate business must embrace all stakeholders indiscriminately." Truly for companies aspiring success in today's compassionate economy, compassionate strategies provide the most forward-thinking path.

Thus, a compassionate lens does not blur business acuity; instead, it enhances it, illuminating the path towards sustainable profitability and a better world. It's not just about enriching the bottom line but also enriching lives. Let's re-envision strategy with the enlightening touch of TheoZenomics!

Chapter 8. The Mindful Investor: Case Studies of Success

In today's fast-paced investment landscape, a surge of interest towards sustainable investing holds sway. Yet, a very few have trodden the path of mindful investing, a journey where the serenity of Buddha's teachings meets the dynamism of green finance. We present you three enlightening case studies, illustrating that mindful investing is not only possible, it's profitable, impactful, and above all, it harmonizes with our shared responsibility to our planet and its inhabitants.

8.1. Case Study 1: The Virtuous Venture Capitalist

William Peters was a venture capitalist with over two decades of experience. Yet, he grew disillusioned with the short-sighted profit-seeking behavior prevalent in the industry. Seeking a change, he turned towards Buddhism for inspiration and found his way to mindful investing.

First, he began by incorporating the principle of "Right View" into his investment philosophy. He redefined success not just by monetary returns but by the social and environmental impact of his investments. His perspective widened, considering broader societal and ecological benefits when determining the worthiness of a venture.

Second, following the principle of "Right Action", he rigorously screened each investment opportunity for ethical business practices, fair treatment of workers, and commitment to reducing environmental impact.

Lastly, instilling the concept of "Right Effort", he committed himself fully to each investment. This included providing mentorship, sharing wisdom, and helping to overcome the obstacles encountered by the enterprises he invested in.

With this new mindset, William found his investments appeared more successful than ever, in every sense of the word. His portfolio, though initially diminished in numbers, demonstrated substantial improvements in both profitability and positive impact.

8.2. Case Study 2: The Enlightened Investors Group

Our second case study introduces us to the Enlightened Investors Group (EIG), a group of like-minded individuals practicing the Buddhist philosophy of mindfulness in their investment decisions. Their story serves as an example of how combining resources and wisdom can create remarkable synergies in mindful investing.

EIG members followed a detailed code, derived from the Buddhist principle of the "Eightfold Path". Investments were considered only if the venture adhered to the "Five Precepts", such as abstaining from harm to living beings and fraudulent practices.

Returns were not measured solely in currency, but also through the metrics they termed as "Meta Earnings". These included key performance indicators such as reductions in carbon emissions, improvement in employee working conditions, and contribution towards local communities.

They regularly held mindfulness sessions, where investment-related stress was managed through meditation, creating space for clear thinking and informed decision-making.

Their combined mindfulness practice, ethical selection process, and Meta Earnings approach put EIG on the path to considerable economic and environmental success, reaffirming the practicality and effectiveness of their mindful investing philosophy.

8.3. Case Study 3: The Compassionate Corporation

Our final case study takes us into the world of a corporation. Compassionate Inc, a multinational conglomerate, truly embodied the Buddhist principles across all their operations, including investments. Their case demonstrates mindful investing at an organizational level.

Compassive Inc followed a holistic investment approach, inspired by the Buddhist concepts of "Interconnectedness" and "Impermanence". They acknowledged that their business was linked with the wider ecological and societal frameworks, and therefore, their investment choices reflected this understanding.

Understanding "Impermanence", they chose sectors that would stand the test of rapidly changing times. This led them toward investing heavily in renewable energy and sustainable agriculture while divesting from fossil fuels and single-use plastic industries.

Through Green Bonds and Social Impact Bonds, they channeled funds towards environmental preservation and social well-being initiatives. The company set an exemplary precedent, illustrating that with mindfulness and vision, corporations can harmoniously blend profitability with sustainability.

In conclusion, these case studies provide valuable insights into the practice of mindful investing. They show us that applying Buddhist philosophy to the world of investing helps foster an investment ethos that is integrative; considering financial returns, socio-ethical impact, and environmental sustainability as equally important. They reveal that through mindful investing, we can contribute to building a more sustainable and compassionate world, all while creating wealth. This is truly the path less trodden but worth every mindful step.

Chapter 9. Treading the Eightfold Path: Ethical Investment Strategies

Take a deep breath as you embark on an exploration into eightfold ethical investment strategies. These strategies follow a course where profit is balanced by principles, where gain coexists with goodwill.

9.1. Understanding the Concept

Investment strategies, unlike fleeting financial trends, are foundationally solid approaches guiding investors to shape portfolios and manage wealth over time. Ethical investments, or Socially Responsible Investments (SRI), present strategies that consider economic returns while enforcing a strong focus on environmental, social, and governance (ESG) factors. SRI frameworks are typically shaped by a broader set of value-based considerations, and it is here that one finds synergy with the principles underlying Buddha's Eightfold Path.

The Eightfold Path serves as a comprehensive guide for personal development and spiritual growth. Its tenets - right understanding, right thought, right speech, right action, right livelihood, right effort, right mindfulness, and right concentration - offer a holistic roadmap for investors seeking values-based wealth generation.

9.2. Right Understanding

In investment terms, Right Understanding refers to comprehending the nature of each potential asset, its implications on environmental and social elements, and the ethical commitments of the entities you are investing in. Detailed background research, fact validation, and market predictions form the cornerstone of this understanding.

Consciously comprehend the performance of green bonds, the credibility of renewable energy stocks, the commitment of ESG mutual funds, the accountability of clean technology enterprises, and the influence of social impact bonds. It is here you understand the fundamental connection between ethics and economics.

9.3. Right Thought

Right Thought, in the context of investing, requires comprehending the ethical dimension of your investments. Before investing, align thoughts with specific ethical and sustainability goals, such as raising capital for green energy projects or supporting sustainable farming businesses.

These thoughts should resonate with personal values. Meditate on ideas of renewable energy, organic farming, biodiversity conservation, or fair trade practices. The decisions made from these thoughts will reflect your commitment towards environmental sustainability and social equity.

9.4. Right Speech

The principle of Right Speech is translated in investment terms as authentic communication with relevant parties. This includes transparent discussions with financial advisors, shareholders, and business partners about the intention to prioritize environmental and social yields alongside financial returns.

Moreover, advocating for ethical investing and engaging in dialogue regarding ESG standards also exemplifies Right Speech. Encourage businesses to adopt greener practices, be vocal about your support for social initiatives, and foster open dialogue about these critical issues.

9.5. Right Action

Moving from thought to action is a decisive step. Right Action in ethical investing involves actualizing investment plans structured around eco-friendly and socially responsible practices.

This entails buying shares of responsible companies, investing in green bonds, supporting social impact funds, or contributing to community upliftment projects. Always ensure your actions align with sustainable development goals and your personal ethical framework.

9.6. Right Livelihood

Right Livelihood encourages investors to generate income through fair and ethical methods. It means choosing investment fields that contribute to the environment and society positively.

From an investing standpoint, this implies prioritizing investments in companies that value worker rights, engage in fair trade, invest in renewable resources, and prioritize their carbon footprint, solidifying assets that contribute to both personal wealth and global well-being.

9.7. Right Effort

Consistency is key in adapting Buddha's Eightfold Path to investing. Right Effort means continually striving towards maintaining an ethical investment portfolio.

Regularly monitor and evaluate investment impacts, actively divest from any unwholesome businesses, and continuously seek opportunities that dovetail with responsible investment principles. Right Effort ensures that investing practices retain their alignment with broader ecological, ethical, and social aspects.

9.8. Right Mindfulness

Mindfulness, an integral part of the Eightfold Path, emphasizes the necessity to remain aware and present. In the realm of investing, Right Mindfulness involves attentively observing your investment performance and impact. Apply mindfulness when reading financial reports, tracking stock performance, assessing company policies, and exploring new investment options.

Adopt an assertive approach to understanding the implications of each financial decision. Be vigilant and maintain attention to details, always connecting these details back to the broader sustainable and ethical objectives.

9.9. Right Concentration

The final component, Right Concentration, is the ability to maintain focus on ethical goals associated with investing. It signifies a firm commitment to sustainable and responsible investing, despite the flux in market conditions.

Regardless of trends and fluctuations, remain steadfast in prioritizing investments that are ecologically viable, socially beneficial, and governance-enhancing, alongside being financially profitable. Concentrate efforts on cultivating patience, resilience, and a long-term perspective.

In conclusion, ethical investment strategies based on Buddha's Eightfold Path demand a mix of deep introspection and decisive action. The path navigates through understanding, thought, speech, and action, espousing livelihood, effort, mindfulness, and concentration. As we embody these principles, we architect our portfolios to bring heightened harmony between profits and principles, creating a blueprint for a more sustainable world and a greener future.

Chapter 10. Application of Buddha-Inspired Lessons in Modern Investing

Most of us are familiar with Buddha as a spiritual entity who encouraged the pursuit of wisdom, compassion, and inner peace through mindfulness. He viewed knowledge as the path to liberation, a notion we intend to apply to the realm of investing. As investors in the modern world, we can blend these invaluable principles with our financial decisions to create an investment portfolio that is both fruitful and sustainable.

10.1. Embracing the Beginner's Mind

Welcoming every investment opportunity with an open and enthusiastic mind paves the way for discovery and growth. This clearly echoes Buddha's teaching: "In the beginner's mind, there are many possibilities, but in the expert's, there are few". The world of investment constantly metamorphoses; hence investors need to maintain an adaptable and eager-to-learn mindset.

Discovering every nuance of a potential investment, regardless of past experiences or preconceived notions, is crucial. It gives us endless possibilities to explore and inflow of fresh ideas, allowing us to make well-informed and profitable decisions.

10.2. Seeing the Interconnectedness

Buddha taught that everything in the world is interconnected. This concept, when applied to investing, urges us to examine multiple perspectives before making a decision. This means we need to consider the social, economic, and environmental impact of an investment to truly understand its value. This framework inherently supports green investing that thrives on a healthy balance between profit and planet.

10.3. Practicing the Middle Way

Buddha walked 'The Middle Way,' steering clear of extremes. The implementation of this principle leads investors to place themselves between high-risk, high-return investments and low-risk, low-return ones. Striking a balance between safety and growth can often translate to a solid, stable portfolio that flourishes over time.

While high-risk investments can provide impressive short-term gains, they can also lead to significant losses. Low-risk investments may not offer spectacular returns, but they ensure a consistent and reliable income source. The middle way encourages diversification to mitigate risks and optimise returns.

10.4. Cultivating Mindfulness

Cultivating mindfulness is a fundamental Buddhist principle that promotes intentional and focused actions. In the context of investing, this translates into making thoughtful, well-reasoned investment decisions after considering all perspectives.

Mindful investors align their financial goals with their values, ensuring every investment decision positively impacts society and the environment. They respond with grace to market fluctuations, maintaining a long-term perspective rather than succumbing to fear or greed.

10.5. The Practice of Detachment

Another intensely profound lesson Buddha offers is of detachment. For investors, this doesn't mean disengaging from their investments. Rather, it encourages us not to obsess over market trends or individual investment performance.

Detachment prompts investors to drop the unrealistic expectation of every investment being successful. Investing is a process of hits and misses. It allows for patience and calm in times of market uncertainty, focusing instead on long-term performance, market research, and constant learning.

10.6. Living Compassionately

Putting compassion at the forefront aligns our investments with causes that make meaningful contributions to society. Many companies working on sustainable and renewable projects are not just solving a societal problem, but often offer great value. Compassionate investments, therefore, reflect an intersection of good business and societal value creation.

10.7. The Power of Patience

Buddha often emphasized the virtue of patience. In an investing context, patience translates into a long-term investment philosophy. Instead of focusing on immediate profits, mindful investors play the long game, allowing investments to mature over time and deliver superior returns.

Chapter 11. Conclusion

Applying Buddha's teachings to investing doesn't mean donning an orange robe and renouncing worldly goods. It invites us to focus on sustainability, mindfulness, and long-term strategy, balancing financial returns with social good. It leads to a reinvented outlook on investing that is compassionate, patient, interconnected, and eternally open to learning. With these principles, we better equip ourselves to create an investment portfolio that reflects our values and contributes to a better world. May Buddha's wisdom guide you as you shape your investment trajectory.

Chapter 12. Enlightened Future: Trends and Opportunities in Green Investing

Ancient scriptures tell us that the Buddha once said, "The mind is everything. What you think, you become." This teaching couldn't ring truer in our modern economy. Many of us actively participate in the financial world with a consistent faith in growth and abundance that is often unyielding. Yet, our world grows overcrowded, polluted, and strained underneath the weight of human development. How, then, can we wield our investment potential in a manner that aligns with damage control, as well as with goals of nurture and collective growth?

12.1. An Era of Change

Mankind has entered a new age of ideology, where our understanding of wealth is undergoing a significant transformation. Investments are no longer solely based on economic criteria; rather, there is a growing emphasis on integrating ecological and social considerations into the decision-making process. This shift has given rise to the concept of green or eco-friendly investing – a potent tool in addressing the mounting climate crisis.

Green investing is famously known for its focus on promoting both economic growth and environmental sustainability. What sets it apart from traditional investing is its conscious effort to avoid funding companies that are detrimental to the environment. Instead, it seeks to boost the performance of companies that offer eco-friendly products or services.

12.2. Green Sectors on the Rise

The green economy is expansive and filled with promise. Let's dive into a selection of sectors that not only encapsulate the green investment philosophy but are also showing significant promise for the future.

Renewable Energy: The renewable energy sector includes companies involved in the generation and distribution of renewable energy, from wind and solar power to bioenergy and hydroelectricity.

Clean Technology: Clean technology involves services and products that use sustainable materials and processes to considerably reduce emissions and waste, enhancing the efficiency of renewable energy sources along the way.

Sustainable Agriculture: This sector includes companies focused on farming practices that respect the ecological cycle, ensuring the protection of soil quality, biodiversity, and animal welfare, without the use of harmful chemicals.

Green Building: Green buildings incorporate design, construction, and operational practices that significantly reduce or eliminate the negative impact on the environment and occupants.

12.3. The Power of Green Bonds

Green bonds are an innovative instrument designed to fund projects with environmental benefits. For investors looking to diversify their portfolio while forwarding a green agenda, these bonds serve dual purposes – the pursuit of financial returns and the fulfillment of social responsibility. One of Buddha's central teachings is the concept of interconnectedness, which we can duly apply to our investment choices. By investing in a green bond, you're directly contributing to a collective solution – a powerful act that aligns our financial decisions with our ethical intentions.

The green bond market has experienced notable growth in the past decade, with issuance reaching a record high in 2019. There is a robust interest in green bonds from both investors and issuers, coupled with strong regulatory support across countries. This is indeed a trend worthy of any green investor's attention.

12.4. Tools for Green Investing

In this era of green transition, it's crucial for us to arm ourselves with the right tools and knowledge. ESG (Environmental, Social, and Governance) criteria is observational metrics for conscientious investments. It includes a company's fair treatment of workers, its effect on the environment, and its corporate governance, thus allowing investors to assess the long-term sustainability of an enterprise.

Similarly, we can harness Positive Screening, a process in which investors seek out companies that actively pursue social good. Negative Screening, on the other hand, is used to avoid companies that are harmful to society or the environment.

12.5. Conclusion

In a world gripped by escalating environmental challenges, green investing offers a beacon of hope. It propels us forward on a path of sustainable wealth creation, harmonizing our ambitions of financial gain with the imperative expectations of planetary health.

As we stride ahead in our journey, it's crucial to recall Buddha's teachings of the Middle Way – the path of moderation. It's a reminder to balance our pursuit of material wealth with a deep reverence for planetary well-being. Green investing, in its essence, is about this equilibrium and harmony, nourishing both our world and wealth from a place of wisdom and compassion.

www.ingramcontent.com/pod-product-compliance
Lightning Source LLC
Chambersburg PA
CBHW071038260726
48661CB00007B/3048